HISTORIC
COMMUNITIES

Children's Clothing
of the 1800s

David Schimpky & Bobbie Kalman

Crabtree Publishing Company

HISTORIC COMMUNITIES

Created by Bobbie Kalman

Dedicated to Bobbie Kalman
by David Schimpky

Editor-in-Chief
Bobbie Kalman

Researcher
David Schimpky

Writing team
David Schimpky
Bobbie Kalman
Tammy Everts

Managing editor
Lynda Hale

Editors
Tammy Everts
Petrina Gentile

Computer design
Lynda Hale
David Schimpky

Special thanks to
Colleen Callahan, Gail Cariou and Parks Canada
(for the loan of the dress featured on pages 16-17),
Samantha Crabtree and Christina Doyle (the models
who appear on cover, title page, pages 16-17, 26)

Consultant
Colleen Callahan, curator of costumes and textiles at
the Valentine Museum in Richmond, Virginia

Separations and film
Dot 'n Line Image Inc.

Printer
Worzalla Publishing Company

Crabtree Publishing Company

350 Fifth Avenue	360 York Road, RR 4	73 Lime Walk
Suite 3308	Niagara-on-the-Lake	Headington
New York	Ontario, Canada	Oxford OX3 7AD
N.Y. 10118	L0S 1J0	United Kingdom

Cataloging in Publication Data
Schimpky, David, 1969-
   Children's clothing of the 1800s

(Historic communities series)
Includes index.
ISBN 0-86505-480-0 (library bound) ISBN 0-86505-519-X (pbk.)
This book examines the clothing styles and accessories of children
in nineteenth-century North America.

1. Children - Costume - North America - History - 19th century -
Juvenile literature. 2. Children's clothing - History - 19th century -
Juvenile literature. I. Kalman, Bobbie, 1947- . II. Title. III. Series:
Kalman, Bobbie, 1947- . Historic communities.

GT1730.S35 1995   j391'.3'097109034   LC 95-2398
                                                              CIP

Contents

Clothes of the past

You probably have a closet filled with different outfits. Most of the children who lived in the 1800s, also called the nineteenth century, had only two outfits. One was worn during the week; the other was saved for Sundays and special occasions. Few rural families could afford to have their clothes made by a dressmaker or tailor. They made their clothes from scratch—sometimes even the cloth!

Dressed like adults

In the cities, fashionable parents dressed their children in the latest styles. Their daughters wore fancy dresses with tight bodices and wide skirts. Their sons wore formal suits. Children's clothing resembled the clothes worn by adults.

Children were not allowed to play in their good clothes—not that they could have! Most fancy fashions were too uncomfortable to wear for playing. Clothes, such as those worn by the children on the opposite page, were hot, heavy, and stiff.

More comfortable clothing

In the late 1800s, children's clothing became more comfortable. Girls' dresses and skirts were looser, and boys wore more casual clothes, such as sailor suits and short pants called **knickers**.

(above) These farm girls are dressed in practical everyday clothing.

(below) A typical boy's outfit included a shirt, vest, trousers, and a straw hat.

Everyday clothing

Many children lived on farms, in small towns, and on the frontier. It was difficult to buy or make fashionable clothes in these places. Even when fancy items were available, few people could afford to buy them. Most children wore simple clothing made of material that did not wear out easily. It was important to have clothes that lasted a long time because many children worked hard around the home or farm.

These farm children are wearing the styles of clothing that most children wore during the 1800s. Simple shirts, pants, and dresses were made to last. Straw hats protected the head and eyes from the sun.

Dresses for girls

Girls' dresses were often made of linen or wool. Sometimes linen and wool were woven together to make a sturdy fabric called **linsey-woolsey**. Skirts were loose and long and reached the ankles. A long apron, or **pinafore**, protected dresses from stains.

Boys' clothing

Boys wore long cotton shirts and woolen or linen pants. Some boys wore a simple jacket over their shirt and trousers. On the frontier, boys wore shirts, jackets, and breeches made of soft leather called **buckskin**. The settlers learned how to make buckskin clothing from the Native people.

The trouble with shoes

Although most children had a pair of shoes, parents often encouraged their children to go barefoot. New shoes were expensive, so one pair had to last a long time.

Traveling shoemakers went from settlement to settlement, making shoes for families. They made children's shoes big, so they would last several years. Shoes were seldom replaced before they were much too small. Children preferred going barefoot to wearing their uncomfortable shoes!

Children who lived on the frontier wore home-made buckskin **moccasins**. Moccasins were light and comfortable, but only in dry weather. When it rained, moccasins became damp and clammy.

*This girl is wearing a **pinafore** over her dress. She and her grandmother have carded some wool, which will be used to make her winter dress.*

Farm children worked hard. Their everyday clothes were plain and comfortable.

Jonah's trousers

Nowadays, if we want new clothes, we go to the store and buy them. In settler times, getting something new to wear wasn't just a shopping trip—it was often a community project! Many people pitched in to help, as you will see in the story of Jonah's trousers.

1. These are Jonah's trousers.

2. This is Jonah's mother, who cut and sewed the cloth to make Jonah's trousers.

3. This is Mrs. Harlowe, Jonah's neighbor, who wove the cloth, which Jonah's mother sewed to make Jonah's trousers.

4. This is Old Zeke, the farmhand, who dyed the yarn, which Mrs. Harlowe wove into cloth, which Jonah's mother sewed to make Jonah's trousers.

5. *This is Aunt Mary, who spun the wool into yarn, which Old Zeke dyed, which Mrs. Harlowe wove into cloth, which Jonah's mother sewed to make Jonah's trousers.*

6. *This is Jonah's sister, who used **carding paddles** to fluff up the wool, which Aunt Mary spun into yarn, which Old Zeke dyed, which Mrs. Harlowe wove into cloth, which Jonah's mother sewed to make Jonah's trousers.*

7. *This is Jonah's father, who sheared the sheep's wool, which Jonah's sister carded, which Aunt Mary spun into yarn, which Old Zeke dyed, which Mrs. Harlowe wove into cloth, which Jonah's mother sewed to make Jonah's trousers.*

8. *This is Jonah, who guarded the sheep, which grew the wool, which Jonah's father sheared, which Jonah's sister carded, which Aunt Mary spun into yarn, which Old Zeke dyed, which Mrs. Harlowe wove into cloth, which Jonah's mother sewed to make Jonah's trousers.*

Caring for clothes

People did their laundry once a week. In some towns, women could send dirty clothes to a washerwoman, but most mothers did their own washing to save money. Doing laundry was a chore that few women enjoyed.

Boiling and scrubbing

Settlers began doing their laundry by soaking their soiled clothes in a large tub filled with very hot water. After soaking, the clothes were rubbed with bars of soap and beaten with a large stick to loosen the dirt and grime. Next, the soapy clothes were scrubbed up and down on a washboard. They were rinsed, wrung out, and shaken to get out the excess water. In the summer, the settlers hung their laundry outside to dry. In the winter, the clothes were hung near the fireplace.

Ironing

When the clothes were dry, they were ready to be ironed. The settlers did not have electric irons. Their irons were heated by coals or on the stove. The **flatiron** was one type of iron. It was a thick, smooth chunk of metal with a handle. Most families had two flatirons. When one cooled down, it was reheated by the fireplace or on the stove while the second one was being used. Some irons popped open so that hot coals could be placed inside.

Those darned clothes!

When clothes were ripped, they were not thrown out. They were mended, or **darned**. Work clothes often needed darning. Tiny, neat stitches were used to ensure that a rip would not open up.

Early washing machines were like a barrel with a crank on the side. Doing laundry in these machines was easier than scrubbing clothes by hand, but turning the crank was still hard work!

This kind of iron was filled with hot coals from the fire. Its wooden handle stayed cool while the iron part was hot.

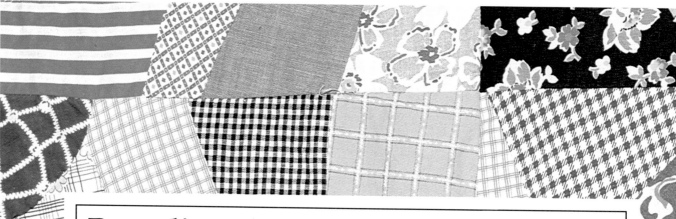

Recycling clothes

You may think that recycling is a new idea, but the settlers were expert recyclers. They did not recycle to save the environment. They recycled because it was easier and cheaper to make things out of old materials than to buy or make something new.

Nothing was wasted

Clothes were always recycled. Some clothes were made from old curtains or flour sacks. Others were handed down from older children to younger brothers or sisters.

Old clothes that were too small to fit anyone or clothes that had too many holes were used to make new things. For example:

• When a sweater was worn out, it was unraveled. The yarn was used to knit mittens, scarves, or socks.

• The material from old clothes was used to patch torn shirts, trousers, or dresses. Buttons were cut off and kept in a box until they were needed again.

• An old stocking stuffed with rags became a soft ball for playing catch.

• Pieces of old cloth could be used to make a loveable rag doll.

• Old clothes were woven into colorful rag rugs. The clothes were torn into strips, and the ends of the strips were sewn together. The long rag strip was rolled into a ball. When there were several balls, they were taken to a weaver. The weaver wove the strips on a loom to make a sturdy rag rug. The strips of cloth could also be braided, coiled, and sewn into a round or oval rug.

• Old clothes were torn into pieces and used as cleaning rags.

• When the settlers made new clothes, there were always pieces of fabric left over. These remnants were saved, along with good pieces of cloth from worn-out clothing. Soon there was enough material to make a patchwork quilt. Several women worked on the same quilt, sewing the different pieces of fabric together. The border of the quilt was sometimes made from new cloth.

• A scarecrow dressed in old clothes resembled a person. This lifelike dummy did a great job of scaring birds away from the fields.

This swaddled baby had a steel frame around its head. If the baby fell, the frame would protect the infant from injury.

The comfortable brownie suit was a welcome change for young children.

Babies and toddlers

The early settlers **swaddled** their babies soon after they were born. The baby's entire body, except its head, was tightly wrapped in a soft cloth. Sometimes babies were bound to a small board that supported their back.

The settlers thought that swaddling helped babies develop straight backs and strong legs. Busy mothers could be sure that their babies would not crawl around and get into trouble. After 1830, very few parents swaddled their children. Most people thought that it was healthier for babies to kick and move freely.

Dresses for toddlers

When babies were a few months old, they started wearing a long white cotton or linen dress. They wore layers of flannel petticoats underneath. A pinafore kept the dress clean. Both boys and girls wore this type of dress when they were toddlers, but boys started wearing trousers when they turned three or four years old.

Brownie suit

In the late 1800s, young children's clothing began to look like the clothing worn by children today. In the 1890s, some parents dressed their children in overalls, which came to be known as **brownie suits**, or **rompers**. Rompers allowed children to play freely without getting tangled up in layers of skirts.

Girls' fashions

When a girl reached the age of four or five, she was ready to wear adult-style clothes. Girls from wealthy families wore dresses made of silk, satin, or velvet to parties and balls. Their gowns were decorated with lace, ruffles, and bows.

Fancy hairdos

Not only did girls wear adult fashions, their hair was also styled like that of their mothers. Girls' hair was tied up at the back in clusters of curls, braids, and loops. Some girls added false pieces of hair, called **chignons**, to their hairdos. Bows, ribbons, feathers, and flowers were used to make hairdos even fancier.

Accessories

Stylish girls wore jewelry and gloves. Many carried small umbrellas called **parasols**. For dressy occasions, girls wore silk or leather slippers. Their everyday shoes extended over their ankles and were buttoned up the side or laced in the center.

(right) **Empire gowns,** *popular in the early 1800s, had high waistlines. They were usually made of thin material. A thicker petticoat was worn underneath.*

(opposite page) This fancy gown was fashionable in the 1820s. The style is called **off the shoulder.** *The young girl is wearing ruffled* **pantalets** *under her dress.*

The shape of skirts

Before the 1850s, girls wore layers of petticoats under their skirts to make the skirts wider. The **cage crinoline** was invented in the 1850s. It was a petticoat that had a dome-shaped frame of hoops. Cage crinolines were lighter and cooler than layers of petticoats, and they made it possible for skirts to be much wider at the bottom.

Bustles

The shape of skirts changed in the 1870s and 1880s when the **bustle** came into fashion. The bustle looked like a leather or wire cage. It was tied around the waist over a petticoat and made skirts look full in the back, especially over the buttocks. Bustles were sometimes referred to as "dress improvers."

More comfortable clothing

In the 1890s, tight corsets and crinolines were no longer fashionable. Girls' outfits were more comfortable and loose fitting. Some parents allowed their daughters to take part in sports. Girls needed comfortable outfits for roller skating, bicycle riding, and playing field hockey. Some girls wore skirts that were divided to look like pants. These pantlike skirts were called **culottes**.

Young girls wore short skirts. As they grew older, their dresses had longer skirts. Teenagers wore full-length skirts. This young girl is wearing a crinoline under her dress.

*Like the crinoline, the **bustle** was a kind of skirt support. It made the back of the skirt stand out. Some dresses had a large bow over the bustle.*

bustle

cage crinoline

This style of dress was popular in the 1830s and 1840s, before crinolines or bustles were invented. Several thick cotton petticoats were worn beneath the skirt.

(above) In the early 1800s, many fashionable young boys wore **skeleton suits** consisting of trousers, a shirt with a ruffled collar, and a short jacket.

(below) In the 1820s and 1830s, trousers and long, belted shirts called **tunics** were in style.

This boy is wearing a long, tightly fitted **frock coat**, a **waistcoat**, and trousers. This suit was fashionable in the 1840s.

Boys' outfits

All boys looked forward to the day when they would stop wearing a dress and start wearing trousers. A boy was usually three or four years old when an event called **breeching** took place. This occasion marked the time when a boy's family considered him to be a little man—even though he was only three or four!

Breeches, pantaloons, and knickers

In the 1700s, boys and men wore knee-length pants called **breeches**. In the early 1800s, however, boys began to wear long trousers called **pantaloons**. At the end of the nineteenth century, short pants came back into style. These knee-length pants were called **knickerbockers**, or knickers for short.

Suits and ties

Throughout the 1800s, the basic suit worn by most boys changed very little. It consisted of a jacket, trousers, and a short vest called a **waistcoat**. Suits were usually made of a dark material. Boys wore neckties with their suits. Bow ties were very popular, but other ties such as the teck scarf, puff scarf, Windsor tie, and four-in-hand tie were also worn.

(above) Both little boys and girls wore loose dresses that were called **shifts**. *Shifts were often decorated with pleats and embroidery.*

(below) Most boys' suits were made of wool or linen.

teck scarf   *puff scarf*   *Windsor tie*   *four-in-hand tie*

Later fashions for boys

In the later years of the 1800s, fancy costumes were fashionable for boys. Many boys had to wear outfits that they hated. These clothes were often tight and itchy. Some boys felt that wearing clothes decorated with ruffles and lace was very embarrassing.

The highland costume

The **highland costume** followed a fashion trend set by the children of the British royal family in the 1850s. A tartan kilt, white shirt, and short, tight jacket made up this outfit. Some boys wore white lace-trimmed pantalets that showed beneath the kilt. Plaid stockings and a matching sash completed the outfit.

Highland costumes were very fashionable in the late 1800s. A small hat called a Scottish bonnet sometimes topped the outfit.

In the 1860s, short, collarless zouave jackets became popular. Boys wore the short braid-trimmed jacket with knickers. The knickers were also decorated with braid.

24

The sailor suit

In the late 1800s, the **sailor suit** was one of the most popular outfits in the world. This comfortable fashion started in England, but it quickly spread to many countries, including the United States and Canada. The sailor top had a large collar and floppy bow tie. It was often worn with knickers.

The Fauntleroy suit

In 1886, Frances Hodgson Burnett wrote a children's book called *Little Lord Fauntleroy*. It was an instant success, as was the suit worn by the main character. The **Fauntleroy suit** consisted of a tight, black velvet tunic and knickers, with a white lace collar and cuffs. Long curly hair completed the look.

Variations of the sailor suit have been worn by children for over one hundred years. Have you worn one?

Few boys could imagine a fate worse than being made to look like Little Lord Fauntleroy! Not only was it difficult to run and play in the tight, velvet Fauntleroy suit, but having long curly hair was downright embarrassing!

In the late 1800s, Norfolk jackets were often worn with knickers. The Norfolk suit was popular for outdoor activities.

Winter clothing

Winter was a difficult season for the settlers. They spent a great deal of time working outdoors. Their houses were heated only by a stove or fireplace, and icy cold winds whistled through cracks in the walls. The settlers valued warm winter clothing—indoors and out!

Wearing wool makes winter warm

Wool was warm and easily available. Mothers and grandmothers knitted sweaters and socks from woolen yarn. A woolen sweater was often worn as a winter coat because it was the warmest article of clothing a child owned. Woolen underwear was itchy, but it kept children warm. Outside, children wore capes, scarves, and mittens made of wool.

Fighting frostbite

Children had to walk to school in the winter, often in deep snow. Since few settlers could afford good boots, parents stuffed straw or newspapers in their children's shoes. Stuffed shoes were uncomfortable, but wearing them was better than getting frostbite!

Fashionable winter clothes

The children of wealthy families wore fashionable winter clothes. Babies and toddlers were dressed in fur-lined capes called **wrappers** to ward off the cold. Older girls wore heavy capes or special flared coats that fit over their wide crinoline dresses. Some girls kept their hands warm inside fur **muffs**. Boys wore long woolen coats, often with matching leggings.

Boys wore masks to protect their face in freezing weather. This scary-looking mask was made of chinchilla, *a material made of thickly woven wool and cotton.*

Gaiters, *worn over boots, kept legs warm and dry.*

During the winter, boys and girls wore woolen union suits *under their clothes.*

Hats for boys and girls

Hats were an important part of every outfit. They were meant to be fashionable, but they were also practical. In the summer, most children spent a great deal of time outdoors. It was important to protect their heads from the sun in order to prevent sunstroke.

Women and girls were especially careful to protect their skin from the sun. It was fashionable to have a pale complexion. A suntan was a sign that a person did outdoor work, which was considered "unladylike." Wearing a hat helped keep the sunlight off delicate skin.

The **poke bonnet** *was popular in the early part of the nineteenth century. It had a large, stiff brim that nearly "poked" nearby people in the eye!*

During the 1860s, girls wore small hats that they pinned on top of their hairdos.

Babies and toddlers usually wore soft cotton or linen bonnets decorated with tucks and ruffles. Babies still wear bonnets today.

Bowler hats, *worn in the late 1800s, had very narrow brims.*

Straw **sailor hats** *were stylish for boys and girls. Some had flat brims and others had rolled brims.*

Some older boys wore **top hats** *like those of their fathers. The top hat was tall with a narrow brim. Fine top hats were covered in black silk.*

The **shako** *had a stiff brim and round headband. It resembles the hat worn by police officers today.*

In the late 1800s, many boys and girls wore flat hats called **tam o' shanters** *to match their fashionable highland outfits.*

At the Valentine Museum in Richmond, Virginia, children helped create exhibits of their own clothes. You can create a similar exhibit at your school.

Make a clothing museum

There are many museums that feature children's clothing of the past. Follow these simple suggestions and make a museum of modern clothes in your own classroom.

Collecting clothes
Each student can choose a favorite item of clothing to include in the exhibit. Make sure the exhibit contains different kinds of clothes. Students might wish to bring a favorite sweater, t-shirt, party dress, pair of shoes, or costume jewelry.

Making a display
To display your clothing artifacts, you will need thick pieces of cardboard. Take each item of clothing and place it on a piece of cardboard. Carefully trace around the clothing with a pencil. Remove the item and then cut out the cardboard shape.

Paint your cardboard cutout a bright color. After the paint is dry, dress each cutout in a piece of clothing. To display shoes, cut the cardboard in an "L" shape smaller than the shoe. Put a sock around the cardboard and place it inside the shoe. Hang the displays on the classroom wall or stand them on a table.

Exhibit time!
Each student should make a label to go with the item of clothing he or she contributed. The label should describe the item, how it is worn, and why that item of clothing is important to its owner. Display each label beside the object it describes.

Your museum is now ready. Invite other classrooms to visit. Plan a day when your parents can view the exhibit.

Glossary

artifact Anything created by people, especially an object of historical interest

bodice The close-fitting part of a dress above the waist

breeches Trousers reaching to, or just below, the knees

buckskin A strong, soft, leather made from the skins of deer or sheep

chignon A piece of false hair worn by women at the back of the head

complexion The appearance of the skin, particularly the skin on the face

culottes A skirt that is divided into baggy legs

embroidery The art of decorating cloth with designs, using a needle and thread

environment The area and conditions in which an animal or plant lives

frontier The undeveloped region beyond a settled area

frostbite A condition in which a part of the body becomes frozen or partly frozen

gaiters Thick leggings that protect the legs and ankles

kilt A knee-length pleated skirt traditionally worn by Scottish men

knickerbockers Short pants that extend just below the knees

linen Cloth made from flax fibers

linsey-woolsey Cloth made of linen and wool

loom A device used to weave cloth

moccasin A soft leather shoe with no heel

modesty piece A collar that covers exposed skin above the neckline

muffs A warm, tubelike covering for the hands, usually made of wool or fur

pantalets Long, lacy pants worn beneath a skirt

pantaloons Trousers

parasol A small, lightweight umbrella used as a shield against the sun

petticoat A skirt worn beneath a dress

pinafore An apron that hangs from the shoulders and is tied at the back

recycle To make waste material suitable for reuse

remnant A leftover piece of cloth

rural Describing or relating to the country

satin A shiny woven cloth

tartan A woolen fabric with a plaid design of Scottish origin. Tartans are a part of traditional Scottish clothing.

tunic A long shirt

washboard A grooved board on which clothes are scrubbed

washerwoman An old term for a woman whose job was washing clothes

whalebone A hard substance that comes from the upper jaws of some whales. Whalebone was used to stiffen corsets and fans.

wrapper A fur-lined cape for babies

Index

Acknowledgments

Photographs and reproductions
Abby Aldrich Folk Art Center: page 18
Colonial Williamsburg Foundation: page 15
Marc Crabtree: cover, pages 16 (both left), 17 (both), 21, 26
Bobbie Kalman: pages 16 (right)
A. Konstantopoulos/Old Sturbridge Village: page 4 (top)
Diane Payton Majumdar: pages 12-13
Thomas Neill/Old Sturbridge Village: page 4 (bottom)

New York State Historical Association, Cooperstown: page 22
Upper Canada Village/Parks of the St. Lawrence: page 7 (both)
Katherine Wetzel/Valentine Museum: page 30

Illustrations and colorizations
Barb Bedell: cover, pages 8, 9, 10, 14 (top), 19, 20, 22, 23 (bottom), 24, 25, 26, 27, 28, 29
Sarah Pallek: title page, pages 12, 13, 16, 23 (top)
Hilary Sandham: pages 7, 14 (bottom)
David Schimpky: title page, pages 5, 6

1 2 3 4 5 6 7 8 9 0   Printed in the U.S.A.   4 3 2 1 0 9 8 7 6 5